God's
Green
Earth

God's Green Earth

NOELLE KOCOT

WAVE BOOKS

SEATTLE & NEW YORK

Published by Wave Books

www.wavepoetry.com

Copyright © 2020 by Noelle Kocot

All rights reserved

Wave Books titles are distributed to the trade by

Consortium Book Sales and Distribution

Phone: 800-283-3572 / SAN 631-760X

Library of Congress Cataloging-in-Publication Data

Names: Kocot, Noelle, author.

Title: God's green earth / Noelle Kocot.

Description: First edition. | Seattle : Wave Books, [2020]

Identifiers: LCCN 2019030182 | ISBN 9781950268030

   ISBN 9781950268023 (trade paperback)

Classification: LCC PS3611.O36 A6 2020 | DDC 811/.6—dc23

LC record available at https://lccn.loc.gov/2019030182

Designed by Crisis

Printed in the United States of America

9 8 7 6 5 4 3 2 1

First Edition

Wave Books 085

THIS BOOK IS DEDICATED TO

JOSHUA BECKMAN

ANTHONY MCCANN

MATT ROHRER

MATTHEW ZAPRUDER

AND

HEIDI BROADHEAD

God's
Green
Earth

The Work

Inside a straight line,
There is solace.

In water,
There is a small gift.

The heart's souvenirs
Pile up under the tongue.

It is easy now
To do the work,

Always becoming
A scent on the path.

Pemberton

That was the promise, a triumph
Of the soul. I still believe that. The
Waters are delinquent, the rivers
Unfold and unfold. A heron's unreadable

Ink, the coast of whatever rearrangement
Happened to us in our bright petal
Coats hung around the half-light of the
Stars. A hand so deliberate, an energy,

A drum. Is this the end of your empire,
Or is it just the world, coming as it is?
What I want from this town is for you
To have joy, the evergreens of your little

Floral shop. The sky unrolls onto a vast
Expanse of spring dirt, and you go on sparkling.

Radio Stations

A dollar in the sand dunes, on Debussy's
Birthday, no less. Better get this to Future
Scripts. These fine surges of torrential
Probabilities, the luxury of submissiveness.

Here and there, your herbaceous feet flow
Like the wind. Harpoon the tongue. There.
I am the fetid world in a glass full of pouting.
Pansies are poisonous, they jerk to the

Sameness of the forgotten dead. I carry
The mother lode on my back, don't say
It unless you really want to. Behind the
Neck is a veil, recombining pictures of

Magic and good old frugal claims. I
Spend my time buying up radio stations.

Paying Attention

He is not doing well. She is not
"Doing well." They are not doing well.
And so the new day blooms with its
Frills held tight across the window.
If I could know that which resembles
Me, if I could taste the insistences
Of dusk, I would rise from the shocked
Grass and imagine a shelter of miniature
Tides. Trouble always follows me. If
I left for some other clime, I would
Be confronted with the sparkling repose
Of hours for a little while, and then
The hammer would come down like
The sides of a city avenue over me.
And so I stay, oh, I stay, and I report
The greenness of the alphabet disappearing
Over my faded jeans. X, you
Have witnessed every disaster, and I know
You know it's true. Still, that is no reason
To stop running, like an untraceable phone.

The Exorcism

A prolonged nap, then a silence. It still
Perches on my brain, how the body grew
Inflamed. The languors of eternity, this
Roadside cocoon, the exotic personhood

Of one so greatly afflicted. Airbrushed
Consciousness, the demons possessed us,
And we overcompensated with kindness.
If we could deconstruct chance, the fulsome

Moon would obfuscate these children,
All happy in the waters. How did it happen?
We got too close to a fire. Our dream pillows
Did no good. A plenitude of imaginings,

What "opens you up"? Numbers freed from
Their clock tick around irreversibly.

Trappings

This shade is deafening.
The river, as it ebbs

Sings a pretty song.
Veils over the city, I

Gather up my skirts.
It is not too late for joy,

And the mornings with
Their sleek trees at the edges

Of metallic grass, striped
With rainwater is all blurry.

I long to tell you of these
Floods that once were.

Nostalgia

Ahead
Or
Behind
The
Thinking
Places
Aside
The
Whirring
Referent
With
Its
Visible
Effort
And
Collective
Globe
Of
Oktober
I
Wish
For

Other
Climes
And
Yet
And
Yet
OH
It's
Worth
Repeating
And
The
Birds
All
Flew
Off
Somewhere
And
Landed
Their
Tiny
Heads
Cocked

Shia LaBeouf

It's funny how Shia LaBeouf
Makes his entrance.
It's funny.
And it's funny how Conan
O'Brien talks,
Really funny.
And at times, Margaret Cho
Can be funny,
Though not always.
It's funny how God arranges
Things,
And we take them all so
Seriously,
When really, so much
About life is just amusing.
I think God is amused
With us a lot of the time,
As we are with our pets.
See how even this cat
Is self-absorbed,
See his bent tail floating
By! Love & forgiveness

Is one thing,
But to laugh is also divine,
And I'll bet Jesus
Has the best sense of humor
Of anyone.
And the little bugs on the patio,
And the little bugs on the patio,
Arrange themselves
Into tiny X's.

Grass

Bowwow to my betters! The
Concern is for stiffness in the wind.
I give you my capture, and a fancy
Gong rings out with its insistences.
Tell me a story—how spring thrusts
Up into the stratosphere, how we
All sat at that window like beautiful
Monsters. I give you silvery trinkets,
And I don't ring out as the splendor
Rises. Too late—I've already given
Everything, and now I'm covered in grass.

Transitions

Grind of the dumped, what I wanted from that
City! Being in the presence of pure love, then
Coming back, is disappointing. Repetitive, broken,
How to tell it all, how to relate back to the highways

Folding up, radiant. So now I know, there is an
Afterlife. I've known for a month, but could only
Tell a very few. Dirty, shattered, this world has
Seemed a void to me, a lick between skin and spirit.

Listen, I am human, but everything is upside down,
I don't know how to tell it anymore. The firmament
Leaks out gasoline, how strangely blurred everything
Is! There is a pure fog covering us now, and I really

Don't know how to go back to the other age fluttering
Behind us. Trying to understand, trying to relate,
I fail miserably in the dissembling moment. Music
Plays all night, and I go on pretending I don't hear it.

The Joy of Living

Unreachable shine of language, pouring—
You can almost drink it! Today I came back
To the dreaming sleeves that drape my mind
With neon. Scrim and claw of enamel words,

Joe fixing the computer, I'm standing here,
Shaking with joy, and my fragile armor is
Turning into flame. Grass thickened by night,
Thrill of this flesh this adrenaline, the bones

In me are only vanity, objects marked with
Cloth. Give me something durable, the pitted
Screens straining the last winter through
Them, and I will give you heaven ringed round

With shame or pride, and sit at the foot of
Things, that rug that holds my shadow for forever.

Redemption

A tree grows
Inside me

(not an Orphic
Vision).

This tree makes
Me sneeze

(Not regret).

The uncaused
Field

In which it
Lies

Is fertile.
Come to it,

Like the dream,
The horizon

Of clouds
Will remain,

But oh!
The sun also

Pretends
Your love of it.

The End of Dignity

Cold slides over the sill. What
You have left behind, all those
Bags of leaves and shit, rapture
Of embarrassment and slow-
Going. Unencumbered by promises,
You go the other way. I stay with
You awhile, the river blowing over us.

Fourth Day Awake

Green seas of holy rice. Denial has broken.
But what of the little helps, the eyes of mercy
That waited in another dimension? I was worried
About exile. I was worried about breakfast.
In the failing light, empty fields. My Sunday
White gloves coming apart at the seams. This
Fragrance that shocked me—oh, at first I was
So angry. As we grow up, though, we learn
Of the love that is most suitable. You did a good
Thing, people, by calling me by the wrong
Name. The harsh elements I have resided in
For almost half a century are somehow a pleasure.
In the middle of the world now, in the recesses
Of love dying out, I will make some music. I
Am beginning to like what I hear on your air,
The silence we tangled in each other's kingdom.

Retreat

Struggle of the twin flame,
Paradise is a hound baying.
And if the tall buildings will
Remember me, I think I will
Become a white village on
A winter afternoon. Yes and
Yes. The rain shining on my
Face, I am blanched by the
Morning, and I praise all that
Is gray. It's the mode, not
Necessarily the essence, that
Drives me. And if I do not
"Grow," maybe I will expand
As I cool. The loud sound
Of the clock ticking, the
Forest beyond the seeds.
Take my word for it—this
Machinery of salt & earth
Is slowly writhing. Spirit
Toppling down, milk in the
Coffee, the day taunts me

With its promise, and the
Night, beautiful and cold
Is that word translated into
Something faraway and warm.

There Is a Darkness over the Land

The soggy mountains, the ecstasy—
Brutal renderings while I get even
With the lettuce crisping in the bin.
Anarchic flowers simply burgeoning

From the piano. This place is a mystery.
This place will maul you into an even
Deeper mystery. Hanging my head
Over a thousand paper cranes, glorious

Light streaming down—I can count
On one hand the times I have really
Hurt anyone. Simple. To finish last
Is the hare's fate. To finish first is

No one else's business, and I really
Can't care if that's what you're trying
To extract. What teaches you is this
Dissonance. Repeat it. Repeat.

Letter to the
Reverend Jane Brady

Sickle-cell November sky, the way the bones
Chip at the mention of evening. What I once
Was crumbles at midnight. Hiding beneath these
Blankets, rosary said, cats fed, I try but I can't

Find sleep. No further from the cross was I,
And it was like a lovely bird offered me something.
The shoulder of the wind nudges by, and I concede
The answer. The corn is not high, the thistles

Not light anymore, I have stopped counting the
Days. Papery things fall from my hands, and I
Stand by the Hanover Street Salon, a four-leaf
Clover in my two fingers. I am proof of the

Survival of trees, bending in the wind, but never
Breaking. Salvation, revolution—it all gets
To me so personally, like poetry, like energy,
Like news that never was, and like truth stripped

Of all its accouterments, and vague thoughts of home.

Groping toward the One Thing

A dark wafer—bing!
A light-green bug—bing!

And the hidden treasures
And the watched bread
And the lovely nuance of the sky's
Cheesy potato head,

Love is a lunatic
Marching down these empty streets
Like a ruined sage.

Breakfast in Bed

He made the funny face. I have diarrhea. Rain
Beats on the roof of this house, and even the

Statuary is unhappy. Keyless, I wander hither
And thither. The yards shrivel up. This is where

My thoughts are sleeping. Afterglow of nodding
Off. I gave my mother a crater on Mars. We

Know how the universe will end. There will be
Some blinding lights shooting through the Tree

Of Life, and I will have breakfast in bed.

What I Want to
Tell You but Can't

Brain held together by domestic beasts,
It is fashioned, they say, out of privilege.

There is no "ideal environment." Even
The landscape of spring is indifferent, and

These wet stones will soon be in the middle
Of a blue fire. Blooming dill, blooming

Chives, is it snowing when you leave? Your
Hands whisper to the animals. A lone

Horse splashes around in a little sea, and
We stand outside, beginning to unravel.

The Visit

The little summers. The towering magnitudes.
No. That was very self-important of me. I'm
Just lonely is all. Scantily clad, the skin of the
Stars unwraps. The girl waits on the other side

Of languid. Steadily, the death of the life goes
On and on. The immensity of wind is
Just a color. I am having an affair with Spain
From far away. Gone, gone is what terrified

The snow. Who is excellent will fall like a
Steady rain. Victories are not easy to come by.
The chives are flourishing. What was that
Feeling of guilt you carried with you everywhere?

The inside of a little ghost. A fathoming, a
Lie in the seeds I held between my fingers.

A Kind of Refuge

Gimpy staircase, the smell of forgetting,
How we fussed and studied these saline
Nights, petrified to a permanent vine. I

Have always preferred to ask how one
Can be forever bodily, how we want so
Badly to intensify the form. Ruined days,

The forms all passing into nothing, these
Lavender flowers and their furious alertness.
One disturbs the wind, one blinks a little

At a time. You are the minute that registers
On a screen like the one lit up before me
Now, you are flight, you are that silence

Of a snowy morning where thinking is
All the action that is needed. A singular
Part of us, sharp and clear, turning numerous.

The Ghost

Mechanical beauty
        of sunrise collapsing.
The three days of peace
        I had last winter
That fox buried
        in its tan hole
Unobtrusive autumn
        with black strands of rain

You are not even a memory

You have been blotted out
        with a green fur X
And stand lonely somewhere
        my well-loved ghost

Pressure Belt

I can't remember the days,
Nor the weeks or months
Or hours,
Or the conversations I had,
Nor with whom.
If you don't believe me,
Take a walk inside my head.
Everything is an eternal present.
If I am angry with someone,
I have forgotten who.
If I am sad, it's all tucked away
Somewhere.
The only thing still with me
Are the imprints of love
On my soul,
And all the strangers who
Put them there
Are like one big stranger,
And I, the animal without
The twig in its placid mouth.

The Secret Place

Looks fine to me now. The creatrix
Sulks around like a bag of beans. I'll call ya!
In the garage, freezing my ass off, I actually
Smoked this thing. I'm a student of language;

Now I'm friends with my phone again. The
Way that cat took his compounds—astounding!
On fire with lunar night! Retrograde, are
You ending soon? Don't start with me, okay?

The ravioli are so dry, the leaps of faith and
Fortitude kill me. I live my life without much
Avarice, but every now and then, I use some
Force, and to avoid any unnecessary remorse,

I always make sure that I check for lice.
O God, keep me in that secret, secret place.

The Outcomes

Solitude can be compared to a lamp
That fucks. Telepathy. Aging. It's
The same thing, this barreling down
The limpid avenues. You dissect the

Monster. The cat is not well. How
It winked and cooed just yesterday!
You are "transparent." You are "articulate."
How then under the mobile stairs

Will I ask a favor of the coffee breeze?
Come here, angel. You were never
An impersonator. The sinister plots
Directed at me only, the nourished

Remnants of pride. Something is
Smoldering in the barn, the outcomes varied.

Socializing

I hate "socializing." Do you hate
"Socializing"? No? A blur of bees
Whizzes by. Love suffers long and
Is kind. The skies spilled on aurora

Borealis, those who love the personal
Will make gestures to sell it. You
Are out thinking in the fields. Your
Tag team loyalty breaks over the

Breakfast. In the executive bathroom,
There are no towels. Notice how
You almost always feel better after
Taking that pill. I need some ointment.

Later, they'll review that book, and
I'll laugh at the makeout party beginning.

Wood

A nun's shadow blackens the dirt.
Nike and Sheba fucked then fell asleep.
The world is square and filled with angles.
The inner relics of another age slog on.

Thoughts hang on the door, and the
Men stand around in studied groups.
Needless suffering is the answer, waiting
To be born. I'm sending a message

To the past: no one's home, and the
Branches that turn in the light speak
Of indignation. Such is the solace
Of the sun. The extremities of approval

Are accumulating grace. We are made
Of wood, I say, and then, I thought I died.

Poem for _____

Fall wind through the treetops,
This creek, which once held a
Dead body in an orange parka.
I have walked here, strangely
With my neck out, cradling
The forms in globes of breath.
How could I cradle that bird,
How could I dance in the half-
Light in the loose world? The
Harbor is carrying me, and I
Am still solitary. The pearl-
Bright October light beckons
Me to someplace else, and
Yet I walk myself, unchanged
By the indifference of the morning.
I give you this: Tomorrow, the
Rearrangement of what has
Been lost gathers up like my
Tattered skirt, and I emerge
With a gift to give you, you
Who are so far and boundless.

Red Megaphone

How certain is it? The napkins we
Write on, the stuttering misplacements.
It's stupefying, really, when we consider
The golden source. Make a wish.

There. See how it floats to the surface
Along with the dead fish. Do you have
A hemorrhoid? Because you're sitting
All funny. I can't get the server off,

Mutter, stutter. It's easy to say,
I am one with everything, but difficult
To say, I am one with separation. Lulu
Cries into the night. Night said

Something through a red megaphone.
If you listen, it won't be that terrible.

Narcissism

Blankets out of focus, see how nicely
You are playing with the other kids!
Lifting a hammer, the hapless weather
Rings. The end has run its course again

And again. The ribboned mind, it takes
Me longer to tell you this than I want it to.
Something is moving—I think you understand.
The flotsam strewn under this compromised

Heaven, the tamping down of a widow's soil,
A delicate skin around these black lines. Put
It all in a box and send it away. You'll be
Glad you did, and the storm that is forming

Itself out of ashes bears the scent of charcoal.
To hobble out of a singular verb, that is called life!

Kitchen

Look at this kitchen!
There's an apple on its head!

And the cracks of my teeth,
And a uranium cloud,

Into the earth—
Somethin' horrible!

Look at this kitchen
In its bright survival.

Look at this apple
Starting to shrivel.

I See Your Face before Me

The sun's molecular cry, white shirts

At midnight. A shower of silver coins.

Heavy ground underneath what is

Contained and marked, as soon as I lower

Myself to the demarcated veins. All

Can be dazzling again. The world doesn't

Grow dark with reasons which

Are separate from what we find. What

I think is most amusing is probably

Of the light. Oh, it is an early portrait,

A letter not addressed, perhaps

"Private" is the sum of what has come to pass.

Ode to John Cage

The others seem more random,
Less intentional. The other what?
Oh it is a textual context, a beatitude
With no friends. The nuclei of meaning
Is closer to the original than just
Taped pictures. Word events. Performances.
Spontaneously or deliberately,
I walk in a way that captures your
Personality. What is freely written are
The spiral nebulae of chance-selected
First lines. Acrostics, fevers. I give you
The names of the kinds of light.

Autobiography

I have slid from miracles

All my life.

Riding the incalculable

Brain waves,

Soaring faster into a bin of light,

I have exceeded the longitudes

Of my yearnings,

Opened an aperture to the bastard

Stars.

In the force field of my dependency,

In the forfeiture of my depravity,

There stands a single blessed candle.

I know better than to blow it out.

The world knows me better than even this.

Paris

The impulse to walk away—how

Can I just let it be like an expensive

Watch? Mottled impossibility, the permanence

Of it! What can't be seen, what can't be

"Occurring." I'd like a more substantial

Perspective, one with cantaloupes filling

An aqueduct or something stupid like a

Stupid boy or girl. I went down the boulevards

In Paris once, and it was leisure to see

The signs painted and toppling while I had

Dinner and a drink. Liar, you never went

There. The ordinary marvelous immersion,

Totally obedient to form was only a turn

Of the heavy neck on a current too blue for me.

Church

It feasted with the others, until
Its entrails were flat.
It told the truth with every course,
But it left out the details.
The curtains moved around
A woman's velvet arms.
I don't see what this has to do
With me,
But I admit I'm kind of interested.

Talking about Beauty

Moments of transcendence evaporate.
I looked so forward to that kiss, that
Vulnerability of particulars. How are we
On this broad principle, sneaking past

A generation? My neck restores me in
A darkened mirror. Daft afternoon of
Triangles—they break the small of my back.
Here you are, disparate, and the slow

Heat marks its course. Pressing forward,
I give you some "discretion," I wait before
The hush of lamps turned off. Where is
Your cave? My arms reach back toward

A tattooed armor. Conceive a notion: I
Will stand back in the tiny rain, howling.

What I Wanted to Do

That vague phantom was supposed
To say something. Obscene passages,
The dull-witted allegiance to ruin.
Desolate fields, speeches that go on

For too long—this is my town with
Its dogged actuality. Someone's intimate
Collection is scattered to the core.
Smoldering moments of apprehension,

A light for a cigarette. The waters
Of Lethe go on as I pick my nose. We
Have traveled over a literal gong, and
It's what you can never bring back,

Live insistences like flowers sprouting
In the shade, my blessing blooming like foam.

Gift

Is there a crisis? So many faults. What's the
Big fucking deal? Body glaring over the Seine,
I think that it's simply what could be done. The
Phenomenology of another day, how well did

You know my hands? Lushly dark, filled with
Gestures, the greed of giving myself to you has
Got me going back to my mystical beginnings.
I don't remember who bought the drinks, but

Somewhere, a little neighborhood café teems
With iridescent atmosphere. The birth pangs of
This molting, the arrival to this rocking chair,
When thought goes to sleep, poetry is the only

Currency you have. Those stars fastened to the
Gate are going out. Take this, it's meant to be a gift.

The Body

Body. The sick body (boring),
While the well body clucks like a timepiece.
The blood inside, the geometry of
Breath, how we don't lose the threads

Of our unbeing. Everyone speaking
At once, this dire exactitude, no longer
Itself. Here, I have something to give you:
It's very small and it longs for a body.

You can have this thing as the spirits
Say anything in the mist just to keep
It going. It goes. It doesn't die or rise,
And between worlds, it hangs like a moon

Over a bird-infested sea. We mark our
Things, and simply go on with our breathing

Reverence

We have joined each other like
Umbrellas, the music in the rain,
The washed-out decoys bright in
My mind. Brother, how many times

Will I say, I am fine, and believe it with
You until it comes true? A plate slides
Off the table. Branches graze this
House, where I sleepwalked last night.

It all reminds me of history that I
Have forgotten, the long tales of triumph,
And the defeat in a lighter time of
Year. I have nothing else to give, maybe

This empathic rain, maybe these fictive
Circuits of breath, the volume a bit lower.

Parents and Children

Cocktails & reindeer, the divine is
Really lost. We are more alive and more
Dead at the same time. No one likes
To talk about this. The young lovers' bodies

Entwine, and drunken, we fall down
Beneath the golden eaves. I did not ask
For this. Yet I did consent, it doesn't matter
When. Our salt ride is now over, and the

Whinnying starts again. Someone guessed
It long ago, saw the simple in the beautiful
Complexity of it all. Will the casket be
Closed or open? Because it might be my own,

Even though I drink in life like a cat lapping
Freshest water. What could any of us do,
Except lie here in the orchard crossed with
Snow, feel the sun on our turned-in shoulders.

The Epic of Gilgamesh

HUMBABA

My friends, who can reach heaven?

The monster bellows like a river swollen with flood.
Many are consumed in his fiery breath.

My friends, who can reach heaven?

Let us ask the mountain for a sign.
Let us cut the spirits from the cedars.

My friends, who can reach heaven?

To be remembered a man must undergo
The ravages of the eight winds.

My friends, who can reach heaven?

No matter how tall he is, a mortal can never reach heaven;
No matter how wide he is, a mortal cannot stretch over the earth.
Therefore, may Shamash open before my feet the closed road

*

ENKIDU

We climbed the mountain.
It was enough.
We chased wild creatures over the grassy plain.
It was enough.
We planted grain.
It was enough.
We drew water from the river.
It was enough.
We dreamed the same dream.
It was enough.
We left our tracks in the forest.
It was enough.
You were the shield that protected me.
It was enough.
You were the sword and axe at my side.
It was enough.
You were the ceremonial coat that warmed me.
It was enough.
May the mountains weep for you.
Both night and day.
May the wild creatures of the plain weep for you.

Both night and day.
May the fields overflowing with grain weep for you.
Both night and day.
May the pure Euphrates where we drew water weep for you.
Both night and day.
May our tracks left in the forest weep for you.
Both night and day.
May the dreams that now grieve weep for you.
Both night and day.
You were the shield that protected me.
Both night and day.
You were the sword and axe at my side.
Both night and day.
You were the ceremonial coat that warmed me.
Both night and day.

*

UTNAPISHTIM

I can see nothing ahead or behind me.
The darkness is so thick, and there is no light.
I go like a murderer, ravaged by the heat and cold.
Why should my heart not be torn apart by grief?

The darkness is so thick and there is no light.
My friend has returned to clay.
Why should my heart not be torn apart by grief?
I do not want to sleep the endless sleep.

My friend has returned to clay.
There are no stars or sun where he is now.
I do not want to sleep the endless sleep.
Neither my sorrow, nor my pleas, nor the tearing of my hair
    could rouse him.

I go like a murderer, ravaged by heat and cold.
I can see nothing ahead or behind me.
Teach me how to build a house that will last forever.
I can see nothing ahead or behind me.

*

GILGAMESH

I am no longer interested in the sword and the bow.
The Faraway has taught me that I am weak.
For whom have my hands labored?
For whom does my blood beat?

My days will soon be washed away like a face drawn in sand.
I have neither friend nor brother by me.
To speak of my despairing mind,
The icy-feathered gulls shriek overhead.
No blithe heart can know what unhappiness I suffer.

Yet I am resigned to all my losses,
And I ask you, my people, to let them touch you.
Let me brand my searing path across the shadows before your
    eyes.
Look at the fine temple I have built!
Search the world locked within its stones with a smooth hand!
Throw off the ceremonial coats that warm you,
And shroud yourselves instead
In the raging fire of the answers that never come,
In the raging fire of the answers that never come.

*

ENKIDU

What violence has been done to the atmosphere?
See how the stars scurry through the thickets,
Nature's balance broken, and the voices of the creatures
Rise like a spell toward a heaven cast in human fire.

I feel him drawing near; he is anxious to search the world
Buried in me with a smooth hand. I can almost touch his features,
The sunburnt hair curled
Around his toes whispering against my own. And yet what ire
Flames within me when I look upon him in his heart. I who have
    speared
The worst of beasts, who have braved pale seas
As they rose and fell beneath me,
I who have pinned the demons of the night until the haunted
    song of the stricken
Drew its curtains over waves of my pure fury.
Perhaps in this roaring silence, I will embrace the meaning of my
    dream.

*

GILGAMESH

I am tired of the light that dribbles from my voice
So washed in certainty that the days
Will blink like lashes over rich fields of wheat.
I want a place older than the leaves,
Older than these strong walls where the story of the earth is
    carved.
Give me a radiance that broods beyond this temple,

Where the hidden mysteries of life and death rejoice
Wildly together, where man, like a dying animal, does not grieve
After the storms have wrecked his simple
House. I want these things, and yet I will not serve
These idols fashioned out of the same clay
Of which I, myself, was pinched by my mother's rapacious need.
The very god of storms has wreaked into my first breath the
    secret
That erosion takes patience, not unlike the willingness to bleed.

Advent

It was an enormous step backward,
Even though it was very ordinary. My
Name still buried in the stone, the lights
Flickering this way and that. You may
Have understood this as the language
Of the sun, the room emptied of everything
Except a strange cloud. I could go on and on,
I could measure my lips with what is spoken
Out loud. I cross over a damp mirage. I
Give it all back to you this Advent, and set
You free again and again, are you weary
Of saying goodbye? Like my mother's ring,
I stay on the hand indefinitely. What rock
Will you be when you reach for that glass?

Compassion IV

The human realities of the living are now
As close to me as my own—oh, see how
Dusty that plant gets when you don't clean
It! The rippling day is a fabulous lesson,
My pants are too loose, and yet. *Bon nuit,*
Mes cheries! All over the whole neighbor-
Hood, your fluid legs move—you are all
Permission and flounce, and your stockings
Catch in the mere light. Perfection, wholeness
Is what I see now in everyone I touch. That
Day when two men came in from the stream,
Wet, bothered, the windows were blackened,
And the cats ran around. Rain came, but
Also sunlight, and the years of hard living
Dissolved. A blanket of verbs crosses the
Threshold. Poetry, you are mine, and I will
Go anywhere with you. A gap in the mind,
A spangled street, my spine, perfectly erect now,
Chooses these words, yet it is as if I have no choice.

God's Green Earth

My kinsfolk, I am sorry for my pride.
Are any of us exempt from a bumpy
Road? The memory of each moment,
The greenness of phosphorescent cities,

How they lick the wind. With large round
Eyes I look at the world—look at us all
Dreaming like that! Then, a million
Chambers with all of us stuffed in, how

Do we ever foreclose on a menace?
Look at a schoolhouse the color of mud.
See how it tricks itself of its students,
And see what we call a rainbow that

Enwraps all of us in a gigantic circle.
See that blade of grass sprouting up
From a verb, the only one we have
Ever needed, and it is rightly called *to love*.

Acknowledgments

Grateful acknowledgment is made to the following publications where some of my poetry appeared: *Granta, SurVision, Conduit, New American Writing, poets.org, Five Dials, The Wave Papers, The American Poetry Review, Blackbox Manifold*, poems from the chapbook *Sonnets* (Clinic Publishing, UK), and poems from the chapbook *Humanity* (SurVision Books, Ireland).

I would also like to give heartfelt thanks to the following individuals: Charlie Wright, Barb Wright, Joshua Beckman, Matthew Zapruder, Anthony McCann, Matthew Rohrer, Heidi Broadhead, Ryo Yamaguchi, Blyss Ervin, my parents, Jo-Ann and Jack Sleight, Denise Duhamel, Franz Wright, Mary Ruefle, Dean Young, Laura Cronk, all of my teachers and students, prayer partners, Dee, Damon Tomblin, Lizzette Potthoff, Soren Potthoff, Hannah Potthoff and Jochen Wachter, Paul Vlachos, Isaac ben Ayala, Curtis McCartney, Cindy Cuarino, Stephanie Horn, Liz Whiteside, Jane Brady-Close, Daniel Kramoris, Francis Picabia for his beautiful image of solitude and the lamp, heard secondhand, Alex Dimitrov, Steve Berg, Elizabeth Scanlon, Rachael Allen, William Waltz, Anatoly Kudryavitsky, Andrew Fried, Carol Kiyak, Paul Hoover, Jessica Roeder, and my dear sis, Monica Antolik, Timmy, Euclid, Obi, Marlon, Max, Blackberry, Topaz, Liz's brood of cats, Snowy, Santo, Junior, Mayor Griffin, Town Council, Lazarus, my plant, and anyone I am forgetting. May everyone be continually blessed and happy on this long journey called Life!!